I0488284

# Stock Investing:

## Stock Market Investing For Beginners

By

Robert Alderman

ISBN-13: 978-1500368791

# Table of Contents

Stock Investing: Stock Market Investing For Beginners

By Robert Alderman

© Copyright 2014 Robert Alderman

Reproduction or translation of any part of this work beyond that permitted by section 107 or 108 of the 1976 United States Copyright Act without permission of the copyright owner is unlawful. Requests for permission or further information should be addressed to the author.

This publication is designed to provide accurate and authoritative information in regard to the subject matter covered. This work is sold with the understanding that the publisher is not engaged in rendering legal, accounting, or other professional services. If legal advice or other expert assistance is required, the services of a competent professional person should be sought.

First Published, 2014

Printed in the United States of America

# Introduction

If you have saved some money and are wondering where to invest then definitely Stock Market is among one of the best options to get greater returns. If you want to grow your wealth then investing in Stocks is definitely the easiest, most tested and most profitable method for making money. Everybody is aware of the fact that investing in Stocks can fetch you greater returns which is true to a great extent, however, most of us might not be sure on where to begin with. In this book we will educate you on the various strategies to start with stock market investing and how one can continue to invest in stocks intelligently and confidently so as to grow their wealth.

In the earlier days Stock Market Investing was well thought out to be a gambling activity and was purely meant for cream of the crop class of people however times have changed and anybody can start investing in stock markets now. Each one of us nowadays hears about investing in Stocks however only some of us do invest and some don't. In this modern era of Smartphone's, Computers and Web, Stock Market Investing has become quite easy but scary.

The scariest thing about investing in stocks is something like putting all your eggs in a single basket and if by chance the stock value goes down you are going to lose. As every coin has two faces, same goes with Stock market investing, with the scariness comes the most beneficial part of Stock Market Investing i.e. the potential for greater returns if you choose the right stock.

# Chapter 1. First Step

Just before you step into the world of Stock Marketing it is necessary that you make sure that all your finances are in place. Here are some guidelines which will help you ensure that your finances are in order:

**1) Hold a Bank Account with Sufficient Funds for Emergency Expenses:** Make sure that you have a Bank Account which has sufficient funds so that you are on a safer end of incurring at least 3 to 6 months of your expenses. Nevertheless this money should be used only in case of emergency situations for instance if you lose your job or if you need immediate medical attention or all of a sudden your AC breaks down or your car breaks down and so forth. Remember not to consider buying a new toy or going on a holiday as emergency situations. This account plays a very vital role in making you financial secure in case you happen to be a victim of any kind of misfortunes. Rather than having to take credit in emergent situations you will have cash at hand. One important thing that you need to remember here is that whenever you are spending money from this account make sure you reload it as soon as possible.

**2)  Do Not Forget to Clear Your Credit Card Bills:** As everybody is aware of the fact the Credit Cards levy an interest rate of near about 10-30% or more than that. Regardless of the fact that how expert you are as an investor you might end up paying to the minimum of 15% interest over the period of time and thus a better investment opportunity is to pay off the credit card bills on time before you enter into stock market.

**3) Discover your Retirement Accounts:** Everybody is aware of the fact that retirement costs a lot of money and thus the best time to invest in your retirement funds is when you are youth. Ensure that you at least invest 15-20% of your income in 401K plan or IRA. The right time to invest in Exchange Traded Funds or Mutual Funds is the youth age and one should invest in these accounts so as to make sure that when you are at your retirement age half of your accounts will be converted to fixed incomes securities and cash.

The moment you feel that you are financially in place, you are all set to begin with investing in stocks.

## Chapter 2. Beginning Guidelines

Here we have some simple guidelines for you to begin with Stock Investing:

**1)** The primary step here is to have detailed information on the various stocks in the market. When you hit the stock market you will find a wide range of stocks such as growth and value stocks, large cap, mid cap and small cap stocks, technology and energy stocks and so on. You should employ various stock analysis techniques so as to get an idea on various stocks so that you can easily make a decision on what kind of stock you want to invest in. Having decided on the kind of stock that you want to invest in ensures that you know everything from top to toe about that stock.

**2)** You must gather information about the stock that you are planning to buy and keep an eye on the earning history of the stock. Keep in mind that the stock that you plan to buy should have a decent and strong earning history.

**3)** The next important step is to analyze your risk tolerance limit. As we all know that investing in the stock market is all about taking risk so it is extremely important to analyze the capability of taking risk so as to have estimation on how much you can afford to lose and this is going to be the amount that you are going to invest.

**4)** Now you know how much you can afford to invest so try to find out the P/E ratio of the stock you are planning to buy. The price per earnings ratio i.e. P/E ratio is nothing but the price of the share divided by the total value of the earnings. Having determined the P/E ratio you need to calculate the Price/Earnings to Growth (PEG) ratio. The PEG ratio of a stock is defined as the ratio of profit to your earnings divided by the growth rate that is achieved during a specific period of time. It is a safer bet to invest in stock which have a PEG ratio less than 1 or near to 1.

**5)** So all set now you can go ahead and begin investing in stocks. The best way is to select around 20-25 stocks with the help of various portfolio management tools available in the market and keep an eye on them. Make sure that you do not buy more than 2 stocks at a time. Having bought the stocks you must keep an eye on their cycle so that you can sell and buy stocks at the right time.

**Useful Tips One Must Know Before Investing in the Stock Market**

**1**) It is extremely important to decide on your risk tolerance limit before you begin investing in the Stock Market. If you are prepared to undergo a drastic variation of 50% or more in a month or less via individual investments then without any worry you can go ahead and invest in individual stocks. The important concept here is that you might end up choosing a few stocks which might not work out for you and their value could degrade but not to worry there will as well be few stocks that will compensate for the losers (just think of Walmart or Microsoft). Investing in stocks is definitely going to be a bouncy and jarring ride for the beginners as the winners are most likely to exceed the losers so that you can come out far ahead.

**2)** One important thing that every investor needs to understand is that  sober Stock Investing does not require you to do lot of trading .Trust me just try making guess work with the upcoming moves in the market  definitely you are going to enjoy the stock market investing. However if you are keen on making real money then ensure that you choose stocks that are likely to grow over long period of time, buy such socks and hold onto them for years to come. The best thing is that once you purchase such steady growth stocks you need not have to check them every now and then, keeping an eye on them once in a while say checking them once whenever the statement arrives or once in few months or just going through them when you get the annual reports is going to suffice.

**3)** If you have made a decision to invest on a long term basis in that case ensure that you only sell the stocks if

**a)** The company that you have invested in is planning to change their business wherein the company is not likely to exhibit long term steady growth that you are expecting.

**b)** If the place value has become so huge that now it is somewhat risky then you can sell out the stocks so as to spread your finances a little bit.

The key point here to be grabbed is that you must not sell the stock just because its value has declined because it so happens most of the times that great good companies are dragged down for the reason that there is an adjustment happening in the overall organization sector or the overall market.

**4)** If you have started investing in individual stocks but are not able to deal with the fluctuations in that case it is a wise decision to invest in index mutual funds or in Exchange Traded Funds i.e. ETF's. The investment strategy behind these funds is just so simple they in turn invest in huge number of stocks so if there is any kind of drop in one stock it is most likely going to be balanced by other stocks that have a steady growth. It implies that in a really critical situation there is going to be a drop of 30-35% however in most of the cases it is likely to vary between 5-20% annually whether it is up or down and with increased time duration you are likely to notice more number of up years that the drop one's.

**5)** If you are having 2000$ to 2500$ for investing then it is suggested that you invest in individual stocks. A wise investment decision is to look out for the stocks which have a consistent growth over the period of time and have scope for further expansion so as to make sure that your earnings continue to grow. To analyze this aspect you need to keep an eye on the price of the stock it should reflect in the bar chart that the price of the stock has a long, constant and plodding upward slope. If you are so confused on from where to gather all this information then the best source for this is the VLIS i.e. the Value Line Investment Survey. You will as well find several websites online that list out all the previous earnings; however the only drawback is that these websites do not give out the earning history of a company free of cost. You can as well get in touch with the brokerage houses or any other full time service broker if you have large account balances. Getting information from brokers or brokerage houses is not suggested for the beginners in the stock market.

## Chapter 3. Understanding Stock Market The Right Way

Having understood the basics of Stock Market Investing and grabbed the knowledge on some useful tips to become a smart trader, you as well need to know that your job is not yet over. There is lot more that you need to understand about the Stock Market as a trader such as the lingo, language, reports and what not. If you are new to the world of Stock Marketing then it is obvious that it is going to take you several lifetimes to master the stock market, however, we are here to help you understand the stock market in a better way.

There is a lot of mumbo jumbo being used in the Stock Market nowadays and thus it becomes difficult for a beginner to understand the various functions and terminologies of the market. Wondering how to understand the stock market and make the best out of it then read on some important guidelines to make sense of it all:

**1)** The foremost thing to start off as a trader is to have grip on the terminology used in the stock market. You can browse various websites such as Investopedia or the Investor Words to find out the meanings and definitions that you stumble upon when reading the financial times of the newspaper or magazine. Some of the basic terms that you must and should be aware of as a stock market investor are Stock Price, Market Capitalization (generally referred as Market Cap) , Dividends, Yield, PEG and P/E ratios, Book Value, Earnings per share and so on.

**2)** Having understood the lingo and language, you must start analyzing the financial reports of the company whose shares you are planning to buy. The financial analysis can be made by going through their Cash Flow Statements, Balance Sheets, Profit & Loss Reports, Yearly Shareholder Report and make yourself acquainted with all the various accounting concepts involved in here. You must as well familiarize yourself with their directions for growth, in what sectors they plan to invest and grow, what is their market goodwill, what is their brand recognition and loyalty, what are their long term plans and so on.

**3)** The next most important step is to do a little economic research on as to what are a bear market, economic downturn, bull market, depression, market analysis, recession time and so forth. It is necessary for you to have a deep understanding of these economic terms before hitting the stock market.

**4)** The most essential and vital part of understanding the stock market is to have a deep understanding of the various government reports, the outlooks and their analysis. It is a must that you read out the reports that are published by the Securities and Trade commission of the country and make yourself aware of activities such as rising or falling interest rates by the Federal Reserve. These reports will as well familiarize you with any kind of direct or indirect impact on the portfolio of stocks due to any kind of government legislation. (For instance if you would like to hold stocks with the pharmacy companies then you must concentrate mainly on the health care initiatives that will be taken by the government in the upcoming year.

**5)** You must now conduct online research about various stock movements on various financial websites such as Yahoo Finance, Google, etc. You will have to look at the stock tables and do an analysis of the reports so as to familiarize yourself with the functioning of the stock market. The best thing to have a better understanding is to set up your individual trading account online so as to practice stock investing.

**6)** You should read various financial magazines, investor advices, books and newspaper sections that feature stock market fundas. Till the time you get hang of the stock market it is suggested that you play only with virtual money via simulation stock market games and invest only when you are confident enough.

**7)** You should understand the stock market investment basics in such a way that you can invest to get greater returns and steady growth and not just do some kind of guesswork always. The reason being for beginner guesswork can be a little risky in the beginning and frighten you from further digging deep into stock market investing.

**8)** You must understand the functioning of the various brokerage firms, experts in the stock market and brokers and find out what is their contribution in determining the stock price on any particular day along with the seller and the buyer. Explore all the services that are offered by the discount brokerage companies and the full services brokerage companies and try to understand the differences between their commissions and services. Generally discount brokerage firms will provide you with a trading account and will allow you learn and mange things on your own whereas a full service brokerage firm will provide you value with regards to stock advice and stock management so it is up to you to make a decision on which style you are comfortable with. For the reason that you are investing your hard earned money in stocks it is necessary that you prop yourself from the threat and menace of losing your money by applying a piece of stock marketing expert advice.

**3 Key Mantra's Before Investing in Stocks:**

**1)** Make sure that your portfolio is diversified and well managed.

**2)** With regards to Stocks, you must always make non emotional decisions. So when you buy and sell stocks make sure you choose those stocks that are best for your wallet and not for your heart.

**3)** Make use of other peoples work so as to gather a list of all the potential stocks in the overall market.

# Chapter 4.  Stock Market Trading Strategies

Investing in Stocks is definitely proven to be beneficial over Savings Accounts, Bonds and various other Investment options as the research reveals that the long term average returns in the stock market are somewhere between 10 to 15%.The success mantra to begin as a Stock Market Investor is to choose the best time proven method and adhere to it without letting your emotions drop in.

Having read the post till here you might have understood the fact that Stock Market Investing requires making correct estimates and perfect guesswork in order to bring in profits to your wallet from your investments. Now what's important here to understand that every trader has his or her own Stock Market Trading Strategy that is derived from the basic trading rules? Thus after learning the basics of Stock Market Investing it is extremely important for anyone as a trader to have thorough knowledge of the stock trading strategies. It is difficult to understand the various stock trading strategies unless you have good experience in dealing with various market scenarios and have a better understanding of the different finer shades involved in the trade market. Before you can begin with actual investing practices it is essential for you to have a deep understanding of the stock market and following the strategies mentioned in our post will make sure that you have covered all the basics in your research so that you can enter the stock market with confidence.

Here we will outline the various fundamental trading strategies that will be of great help to you in maximizing your profits and minimizing your losses.

## 1) Swing Strategy for Trading

If you are open and flexible with your approach to investment then definitely Swing Trading Strategy is for you. The success rate with this strategy merely depends on the extent of discretion applied by the trader. The principle behind the swing Strategy is that if you hold tradable assets for a specific period of time they are by hook or crook going to generate profits because of the variation ("Swing") in the price of those assets. If employing this strategy as a trader you can hold on to these assets for  more than the day trading holding time and less than the buy & hold investment position which generally lasts for few years.

The best possible time for buying and selling stocks with this strategy is determined with the help of various mathematical rules so that you can easily get rid of subjectivity, any kind of emotional interference or any other manual effort which are pretty common to occur in case of swing trading strategy. The risk involvement with this strategy is completely based on the degree of market assumption and nature of the market speculation that is involved.

**2) Penny Stock Trading Strategy**

If you would like to trade in penny stocks (stocks that are traded at a value of 1$ or less per share) then this strategy will benefit you in determining the best conditions for the same. One thing before you involve yourself into Penny Trading is that the Penny Stocks will not be scheduled on any of the stock exchange markets despite the fact that there is authorization to include the stocks on the list. The reason being the nature of the costs that is linked with these shares, it is the small business organizations which indulge themselves in the trading of these securities. There is considerable amount of risk involved in trading these securities as well the trading volume of penny stocks is also very low however most of the people consider this to be a profitable investment option when it comes to stock trading. It is thus suggested that when you are trading with penny stocks be highly cautious as the low value of these stocks must not confuse your decision on choosing the superlative trading strategy for minimizing the losses.

**3) Forex Trading Strategy**

This strategy is well-liked in the trading market and it as well has several challenges involved due to the value of foreign exchange currencies varying as per the global economic market norms. In this strategy the ideal conditions for buying and selling currency pair at a specific period of time are determined by a set of analytical methods and rules. The Forex strategy is designed by making use of two important aids namely the current events in the market and the recent news that is most likely to have a bang on the foreign exchange rates and various charting tools that are meant for technical analysis.

Experts who have been in the world of Stock Market and foreign exchange since quite some time suggest that in a place where there is a probability of high fluctuations and instability in the dynamics of the current currency market hedging and speculation are a must to plan the trading strategy. It is advised that you make use of various automated trading systems so that you can train the system in such a way that it will monitor the stock market in accordance with your strategic methods and find out what are the most favorable trading conditions for you to buy or sell stocks. If you do not want to implement this approach then a better alternative to his is to hire a person who will manually keep an eye on the minute changes on the screen and then make calculations based on the analysis and changes in the stock value.

Though it is a well know fact that it is difficult to end up choosing a perfect trading strategy as a trader it is realistic and practicable to choose trading strategies that will provide greater probability of profit and be of assistance in minimizing your losses.

## Chapter 5. Success Mantra

You should refrain yourself from investing all your money in a single go rather invest it at a periodic interval of time. Keep an eye on the stock market and sell the shares when the market is at its high and buy shares when the market is at its low. You should make sure that you buy stocks from various sectors in the industry. The only success mantra here is that your success in the stock market will completely depend on your capability to invest money at the right stock price and at the right time.

So if you are having the right strategy in place then you are good to go as a trader. Remember not to worry even if your strategy fails, just change it up. Nevertheless if your strategy seems to be working good as expected, you possibly would want to change it as the stock market tends are not always constant. With so thousands of people in the world of stocks everybody is trying to come up with a strategy to beat their competitor and thus it is at all times necessary to remain updated with latest stock market trends and continue learning the stock market strategies and try finding out the secrets behind them so as to make perfect investment decisions.

## Thank You Page

I want to personally thank you for reading my book. I hope you found information in this book useful and I would be very grateful if you could leave your honest review about this book. I certainly want to thank you in advance for doing this.

www.ingramcontent.com/pod-product-compliance
Lightning Source LLC
Chambersburg PA
CBHW071602170526
45166CB00004B/1764